Journey of Faith

for Advent and Christmas

In the winter, the trees are asleep,
Ghosts of their former selves.
And the snow falls and softly
Blankets them with white.

And I thank you, God, for the
Quiet beauty of winter.

In the spring, the trees awaken
And shake off their white winter blanket.
New leaves appear,
And the winter, black and white,
Dissolves into the bright, cheerful noise
Of spring.

And I thank you, God, for the
New, emerging beauty of spring.

In the summer, the trees
Reach their leaves to the sky in praise.
They sway in gentle breezes
And shade the ground in shadows.

And I thank you, God, for the
Sparkling, sunlit beauty of summer.

In the autumn, the trees turn
Bright yellow and orange and scarlet.
The leaves say their good-byes in
Seas of color, then
Blanket the ground like the snow to come.

And I thank you, God, for the
Brilliant beauty of fall.

For all the seasons and all the days,
I thank you, God, in so many ways.

(Sarah Cannon, in *You Give Me the Sun,* pages 10–11)

Journey of Faith for Advent and Christmas

by Mary Shrader with Therese Brown and Tony Tamberino

 Genuine recycled paper with 10% post-consumer waste. 5103100

The publishing team included Barbara A. Murray and Laurie Delgatto, development editors; Lorraine Kilmartin, reviewer; Mary Koehler, permissions editor; prepress and manufacturing coordinated by the prepublication and production services departments of Saint Mary's Press.

Images © 2005 FaithClipart.com

The scriptural quotations contained herein are from the New Revised Standard Version of the Bible, Catholic Edition. Copyright © 1993 and 1989 by the Division of Christian Education of the National Council of the Churches of Christ in the United States of America. All rights reserved.

The prayer by Sarah Cannon on page 1 is from *You Give Me the Sun: Biblical Prayers by Teenagers,* edited by Carl Koch (Winona, MN: Saint Mary's Press, 2000), pages 10–11. Copyright © 2000 by Saint Mary's Press. All rights reserved.

The "Advent Wreath Blessing" activity on pages 6–7 and the blessings on pages 11, 13, 17, 22, and 34 are from or are adapted from *Ministry Ideas for Advent and Christmas,* by Janet Claussen and Marilyn Kielbasa (Winona, MN: Saint Mary's Press, 2005, pages 17–21 and 85.). Copyright © 2005 by Saint Mary's Press. All rights reserved.

The prayer "Angelus" on page 21 is from *A Book of Prayers* by the International Commission on English in the Liturgy (ICEL). English translation copyright © 1982 by ICEL. All rights reserved. Used with permission.

During this book's preparation, all citations, facts, figures, names, addresses, telephone numbers, Internet URLs, and other pieces of information cited within were verified for accuracy. The authors and Saint Mary's Press staff have made every attempt to reference current and valid sources, but we cannot guarantee the content of any source, and we are not responsible for any changes that may have occurred since our verification. If you find an error in, or have a question or concern about, any of the information or sources listed within, please contact Saint Mary's Press.

Printed in the United States of America

Printing: 9 8 7 6 5 4 3 2 1

Year: 2013 12 11 10 09 08 07 06 05

ISBN 0-88489-881-4

Journey of Faith series

Journey of Faith for Advent and Christmas:
Creating a Sense of Belonging Between Young People and the Church

Journey of Faith for Lent:
Creating a Sense of Belonging Between Young People and the Church

Journey of Faith for Easter and Pentecost:
Creating a Sense of Belonging Between Young People and the Church

Journey of Faith for Ordinary Time:
Creating a Sense of Belonging Between Young People and the Church

Pray It! Study It! Live It!® resources offer a holistic approach to learning, living, and passing on the Catholic faith.

Table of Contents

Introduction

Each year the earth goes through four seasons. Different parts of the country and of the world experience the seasons in various ways. In general,

winter is a time of cooler weather;

spring, a time of new growth;

summer, a time of warmer weather;

and *fall,* a time of change.

Our lives are full of still more cycles, and the school year is a main cycle in your life right now. Each year has time for newness and for change. There is time for routines such as reading, studying, and participating in extracurricular activities. Not-so-ordinary events—big tests or exams and the beginning and ending of the school year—also have time.

January December

The Church also revolves around a **calendar,** much like the seasons, the school year, and the twelve months from January to December. This cycle of Church seasons is called the *liturgical year,* and its purpose is to mark the celebration of the Church's liturgies. The Church calendar begins with Advent (usually near the first weekend of December) and ends just before Advent begins again (usually near Thanksgiving time).

The liturgical year is built around important historical events—such as

Jesus's birth, death, and Resurrection—

in which God's saving power was made real. The liturgies in the liturgical year help us remember God's saving power made real in those historical events.

The Church's calendar includes times designated as ordinary—not surprisingly, these are called **Ordinary Time.** The liturgies celebrated during Ordinary Time include stories and practices that are good for us to routinely pay attention to. The Church calendar also includes special, or not-so-ordinary, times such as **Lent, Easter, Advent,** and **Christmas.**

In this book, we will take a closer look at the seasons of *Advent* and **Christmas.**

Now, take one minute to write down any words that come to mind when you hear the word *Advent.* If you don't feel that you know much about Advent, write down something you have heard someone else say about Advent, or write down some questions you have about Advent that you might hope to have answered in this book.

Advent is celebrated during the four weeks before **CHRISTMAS.** Those four weeks give Christians an opportunity to take time to reflect on the meaning of the Christmas season. It sure is easy to get wrapped up in worrying about the presents you are wishing for or when school will let out for break. But in the midst of life's hustle and bustle, Advent gives us a chance to be

peaceful, calm, patient, and *hopeful.*

Advent offers us a chance to practice thinking about other people. Advent is a great time to think about gifts from the heart, not necessarily from the mall.

This book in the Journey of Faith series will be your companion as you journey through the Advent and Christmas seasons. During this time, you will be reminded of two important journeys: Mary and Joseph's to Bethlehem and the Magis' (three kings) to visit Mary and Joseph after Jesus was born. Their journeys remind us that God is always with us, always guiding us, and always caring about us. That God is always with us is the most important thing to remember as you journey through the seasons.

For each week of the Advent and Christmas seasons, this workbook has corresponding activities that include Scripture **readings,** reflection and discussion **questions, ideas** to think about, and **topics** to discuss with your fellow faith-sharers, friends, and family members. In addition, this workbook has open spaces for writing your own thoughts or for drawing.

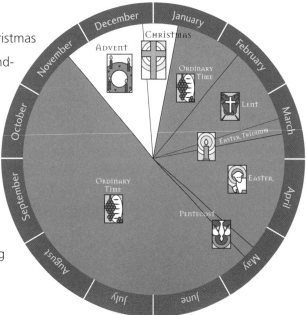

Chapter 1
Have an Advent Attitude!

At times, some of us may be criticized for having an attitude—a feeling, an approach, or a perspective on any given subject. But Christians should have certain attitudes. Advent calls Christians to be joyful, patient, willing, prayerful, and intentional. Advent also includes an opportunity to reflect on our sinfulness so that we can be ready to accept the gift of the birth of Christ into our lives.

Because the Advent season occurs year after year, we have the opportunity each year for renewal, a time to readjust our attitudes. We remember not only how people welcomed Jesus two thousand years ago, but we recall, once again, that Christ is present today. We take a cue from the Scriptures, which invite us to have an Advent attitude of awareness of God's presence in the world and in all people.

READINGS

First Sunday of Advent

- **Cycle A:** Isaiah 2:1–5; Romans 13:11–14; Matthew 24:37–44
- **Cycle B:** Isaiah 63:16–17,19; 64:2–7; 1 Corinthians 1:3–9; Mark 13:33–37
- **Cycle C:** Jeremiah 33:14–16; 1 Thessalonians 3:12—4:2; Luke 21:25–28,34–36

OPTIONAL ACTIVITY

Advent Wreath Blessing

Catholics have traditions for celebrating the liturgical seasons and the story of their faith. One of the most recognizable symbols is an Advent wreath used by churches and families during the four weeks before Christmas.

The wreath—a circle that has no beginning and no end—symbolizes the eternity of God, who always was and always will be. God is the alpha and the omega. We set the wreath in a place of honor just as we keep God in a place of honor at the center of our lives. The wreath reminds us of our own mortality and the everlasting life promised to us through Christ.

The circle shape of the wreath also reminds us that as the earth revolves around the sun and as the seasons change, so too do our lives revolve around God, from whom all life flows.

The four candles used in the Advent wreath represent the four weeks of Advent. The colors of the candles are significant. Three of the candles are purple, reminding us that Advent is a time for prayer and reflection as we prepare for Christmas. One candle is pink and represents the third Sunday of Advent, a time for anticipating the joy of Christmas as the birth of Jesus, the light of the world, draws closer. The lighting of each candle signifies our looking forward with joy and hope to the celebration of the Lord's first coming into the world and the anticipation of the Second Coming, when Jesus will come again in glory.

One purple candle is lit.

Some things cannot be rushed. O God of Love, as we light this candle, we pray for the grace to wait patiently. Your people waited so long for the coming of a savior. We too are anxious for the celebration of your coming. We pray to be ready and alert, always trying to live the life you want for us. We light this candle in the name of Jesus, the Christ, who comes as Light to the world. Amen.

(This activity is adapted from Janet Claussen and Marilyn Kielbasa, *Ministry Ideas for Celebrating Advent and Christmas with Teens, Families, and Parishes,* pages 17–21.)

STUDY IT! Scriptural Attitudes

An Advent Attitude Adjustment

Ten Practices for an Advent Attitude

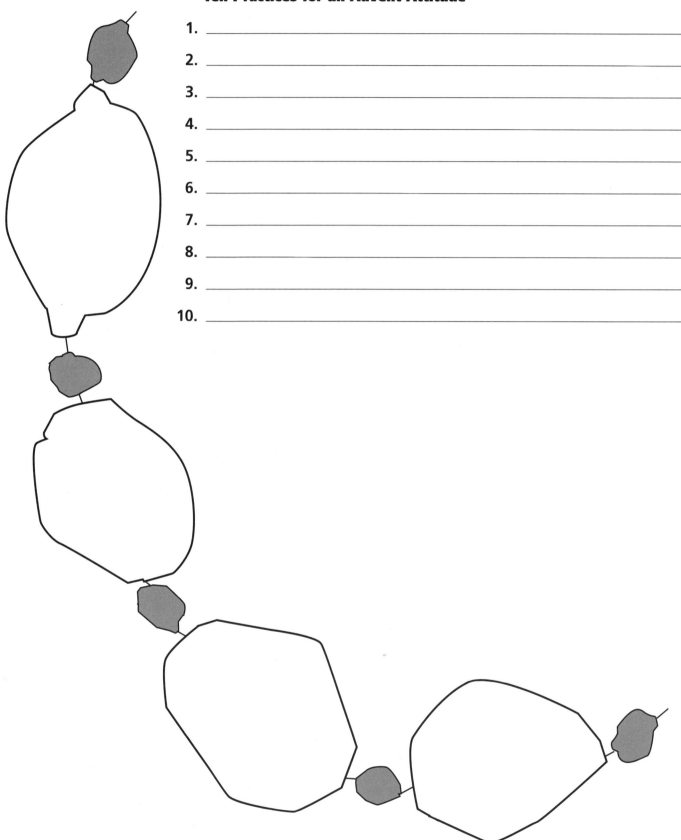

1. _____
2. _____
3. _____
4. _____
5. _____
6. _____
7. _____
8. _____
9. _____
10. _____

Watch While You Wait

Here are five things I am waiting for during Advent as Christmas approaches:

1. _____

2. _____

3. _____

4. _____

5. _____

Here are three things worth waiting for and working toward at this time in my life:

1. _____

2. _____

3. _____

Here is one thing worth waiting for in my relationship with God:

1. _____

Skills for Watching While You Wait
Write two skills you would like to practice as you learn to wait.

1. _____

2. _____

Put on Christ

Prayer for the Spirit of Christian Joy

God of joy and gladness,
look upon us as we begin this Advent time.
Open our hearts and minds to the coming of your Son.
Fill our lives with the Spirit of anticipation
so that as we prepare for Christmas,
we will know the joy of your Love.
Let peace abound and let justice flourish,
that every nation on earth
will shout with the joy that comes through Jesus,
God with us, forever and ever. Amen.

Make Me Ready, Lord

Litany of Readiness

Leader: When Jesus comes again,
All: Make me ready, Lord.
Leader: When my family challenges me,
All: Make me ready, Lord.
Leader: When my friends need me,
All: Make me ready, Lord.
Leader: When I am stressed at school,
All: Make me ready, Lord.
Leader: When I make tough decisions,
All: Make me ready, Lord.
Leader: When my faith is weak,
All: Make me ready, Lord.
Leader: When the parish asks me to use my gifts,
All: Make me ready, Lord.
Leader: When God calls me,
All: Make me ready, Lord.

Chapter 2
Are You Ready?

Through television, radio, and the movies, we are aware of characters rushing around trying to do many things in short periods of time. As Christmas approaches, many people hurry to finish shopping, to decorate their homes and yards, and to celebrate—all before the Christmas season is even here. Advent reminds Christians that waiting and patience are their own rewards. This patient waiting opens us up to the still, quiet voice of God and gives us the ability to look ahead while we live out each moment as fully as possible.

In the Gospels of Advent, we encounter John the Baptist—the last of the prophets whose mission was to prepare the people for the coming of the Messiah—to point to the coming of Jesus. Advent reminds us that we too share the mission of John the Baptist. We are called to be aware of Christ's presence in our midst and to lead others to that same awareness. John the Baptist is a good model for all of us as we discover the value of waiting and preparing.

READINGS

Second Sunday of Advent

- **Cycle A:** Isaiah 11:1–10; Romans 15:4–9; Matthew 3:1–12
- **Cycle B:** Isaiah 40:1–5,9–11; 2 Peter 3:8–14; Mark 1:1–8
- **Cycle C:** Baruch 5:1–9; Philippians 1:4–6,8–11; Luke 3:1–6

OPTIONAL ACTIVITY

Advent Wreath Blessing

Two purple candles are lit.

O God of hope, you sent your messenger John the Baptist who tells us to be prepared. It sounds so easy, yet there are so many preparations and so little time. As our schedules get cluttered with activities this time of year, we light these two candles to remind ourselves that Advent is a gift to us. We pause amid the busyness to prepare our hearts for the mystery and the magic of Christmas. We light these candles in the name of Jesus, the Christ, who comes as Light to the world. Amen. (Janet Claussen and Marilyn Kielbasa, *Ministry Ideas for Celebrating Advent and Christmas with Teens, Families, and Parishes,* pages 17–21.)

What's Worth Waiting For?

- Isaiah 40:1–5,9–11
- Isaiah 2:1–5
- Philippians 1:4–6,8–11

- Jeremiah 33:14–16
- Isaiah 11:1–10
- Micah 5:1–4a

What are the people in the passage waiting for?

What is most important for them to wait for?

Day by Day

In the space below, write anything you would like to remember from your conversation with Jesus during the meditation prayer.

Chapter 3
Halfway Home

The Incarnation, or real human presence of God, is a gift freely given to us by God. No one has to earn or deserve the love and joy that is given to us through the birth of the baby Jesus. So why do we concern ourselves with "preparing" during Advent if the gift of Christmas will be given to us anyway? Our relationship with God is similar to any other earthly relationship in that we will be most fulfilled when we actively participate in that relationship. Jesus calls us to transform the world into the Kingdom of God. We are called to be disciples and to make us and everything around us ready for God's coming into the world.

READINGS

Third Sunday of Advent

- **Cycle A:** Isaiah 35:1–6,10; James 5:7–10; Matthew 11:2–11
- **Cycle B:** Isaiah 61:1–2,10–11; 1 Thessalonians 5:16–24; John 1:6–8,19–28
- **Cycle C:** Zephaniah 3:14–18; Philippians 4:4–7; Luke 3:10–18

OPTIONAL ACTIVITY

Advent Wreath Blessing

Two purple candles and one rose-colored candle are lit.

> O God of light, the days grow short and the lists of things to do become longer. In the middle of all the busyness, your messenger John the Baptist calls us to examine the way we live. May we be prophets in our own time, challenging the status quo as we prepare the way for the coming of your Son. We light these candles in the name of Jesus, the Christ, who comes as Light to the world. Amen. (Janet Claussen and Marilyn Kielbasa, *Ministry Ideas for Celebrating Advent and Christmas with Teens, Families, and Parishes,* pages 17–21.)

STUDY IT!   Are You Ready?

Use the space provided to answer the following questions:

Based on the readings, what do you think we are waiting for? What does the end of time mean?

The Gospel writers are talking about the Second Coming of Christ and the end of time. How does it feel to wait for the end of time?

What do the Gospels tell you about how to prepare for the end of time?

LIVE IT!   Pay It Forward

How am I going to "pay it forward" this Advent?

The Real Presence of Presents

Chapter 4
Joy, Anticipation, Journey, Plan

When confronted by the angel Gabriel, Mary asked, "How can this be?" Various people in the Advent readings, including Mary, the shepherds, Zechariah, Joseph, the Magi, and Herod, encounter God, who had plans for them that changed the direction of their lives. Through prayer, scriptural study, and participation in our faith community, we can better understand what good things God has planned for us. Sometimes we may be surprised, pleasantly or otherwise, with something that was not in "our" plan.

READINGS

Fourth Sunday of Advent

- **Cycle A:** Isaiah 7:10–14; Romans 1:1–7; Matthew 1:18–24
- **Cycle B:** 2 Samuel 7:1–5,8–12,14,16; Romans 16:25–27; Luke 1:26–38
- **Cycle C:** Micah 5:1–4; Hebrews 10:5–10; Luke 1:39–45

Pick a Card, Any Card

Think about how you would answer the following questions and discuss your answers with your partner. After you have discussed each answer with your partner, record your answers to each question in the space provided.

• How would you feel about having to accomplish the task or journey you have picked out of the hat?

• Pretend that you have been told that you have to do what is on the card you chose. Knowing that you did not receive your own card and cannot look at your own card, how do you feel about not being able to accomplish what you wrote down?

• How would you feel about seeing someone else accomplish the task or journey you wrote down?

• Share an experience of someone you know who had to change plans because of life circumstances. An example would be someone who unexpectedly got cut from the soccer team, had to move because a parent got a new job, had a major injury or illness, or received news of a new baby sister or brother on the way.

Advent Wreath Blessing

Three purple candles and the pink candle are lit.

Mary, Mother of God, during the last days when you carried Jesus within you, you must have felt him moving and kicking in his yearning to be born. Help us feel the presence of God within us. We look to you and Saint Joseph for guidance on how to nurture Jesus in our hearts. We light these candles in the name of your son Jesus, the Christ, who comes as Light to the world. Amen. (Janet Claussen and Marilyn Kielbasa, *Ministry Ideas for Celebrating Advent and Christmas with Teens, Families, and Parishes*, pages 17–21.)

"What Happens When God's Plans Aren't Yours?" Talk Show

Review the Scripture reading from the following list for your group's assigned character. Then use the space provided to record the interview questions your group wants the talk show host to ask your group's character.

- Mary (Luke 1:26–38)
- Zechariah (Luke 1:5-25,57–66)
- Shepherds (Luke 2:8–20)
- Joseph (Matthew 1:18–25, Luke 2:1–7)
- The Magi (Matthew 2:1–12)
- Herod (Matthew 2:7–18)

1. _____

2. _____

3. _____

What Would You Do?

Use the space provided to record your responses to the following questions:
What would you do if . . .

- your parents told you the family was going to move?

- your parents couldn't afford to send you to the college you want to go to?

- you had to give up your favorite sport or instrument during high school?

- you felt God was calling you to be a priest, a nun, or a lay minister?

Like the people you heard about in the Scriptures, how are you going to respond when you catch a glimpse of God's plans for you?

Three ways I can be open to and understand God's plans for my life are:

Expectant Church

Use the following questions to interview your parent. Record the answers in the space provided.

- Tell me something about your life before you knew that I would be in it.

- How did you feel when you found out that you would have a child?

- What did you do to prepare for my arrival? What did you buy, who did you tell, where did you go?

- What was enjoyable about preparing for my arrival, and what was difficult or challenging?

- Who helped you get ready for my arrival?

- What hopes did you have for me then? What hopes do you have for me now?

Pray It!

Prayer of Faith and Acceptance

Use the space provided to write a short prayer of faith and acceptance for those times when it seems that plans you have made aren't going to happen.

Angelus

Leader: The angel spoke God's message to Mary,
All: and she conceived of the Holy Spirit.
All: Hail, Mary . . .

Leader: "I am the lowly servant of the Lord:
All: let it be done to me according to your word."
All: Hail, Mary . . .

Leader: And the Word became flesh
All: and lived among us.
All: Hail, Mary . . .

Leader: Pray for us, holy Mother of God,
All: that we may become worthy of the promises of Christ.

Leader: Let us pray.

Lord,
fill our hearts with your grace:
once, through the message of an angel
you revealed to us the incarnation of your Son;
now, through his suffering and death
lead us to the glory of his resurrection.

We ask this through Christ our Lord.

All: Amen.

(A Book of Prayers)

Chapter 5
Let Christmas Speak for Itself

READINGS

Christmas Day

- **Cycles A, B, and C:** Isaiah 52:7–10; Hebrews 1:1–16; John 1:1–18 or John 1:1–5,9–14

OPTIONAL ACTIVITY

Wreath Blessing

The three purple candles and one pink candle have been replaced with four white candles or with one large white candle in the center of the wreath.

The white candle, or candles, is lit.

> Glory Alleluia! Christmas is here and we rejoice with the angels. We have arrived at this moment and our hearts are bursting with the alleluia that Christ is born. God in heaven, Creator of all that is good, you designed the universe. And when all was ready, you sent your Son to dwell among us. Let us savor the season, seeing Christ in one another as we rejoice and live in gladness. In Jesus's name we pray. Amen. (Janet Claussen and Marilyn Kielbasa, *Ministry Ideas for Celebrating Advent and Christmas with Teens, Families, and Parishes,* pages 17–21.)

Chapter 6
Feast of the Holy Family

The Scriptures are filled with God's promise to send the Messiah, a promise that is fulfilled with the birth of Jesus, an event we celebrate on Christmas Day. Through Advent and into Christmas, the theme of giving testimony and bearing witness to God's promise is strong.

Everyone is a member of a family. On the Feast of the Holy Family, we hear about the many members of Jesus's extended family—Anna, Simeon, Joseph—who were influenced and connected to his life in various ways. This chapter will define *family* and *extended family* and address how we are called to live in those connected ways.

READINGS

Feast of the Holy Family

- **Cycle A:** Sirach 3:2–7,12–14,17; Colossians 3:12–21 or 3:12–17; Matthew 2:13–15,19–23
- **Cycle B:** Genesis 15:1–6; 21:1–3; Hebrews 11:8,11–12,17–19; Luke 2:22–40 or Luke 2:22,39–40
- **Cycle C:** 1 Samuel 1:20–22,24–28; 1 John 3:1–2,21–24; Luke 2:41–52

Recognizing God's Presence

God's presence is in our . . .

Receiving Jesus's ultimate sacrifice _____

Focusing our prayer or conversation _____

Using our gifts _____

Knowing we are God's unique creation _____

Gathering as a people in God's name _____

Appreciating all God's creation _____

Desiring to learn and grow _____

Caring about others _____

Seeing good in every person _____

Words to love and live by _____

Using another form of prayer _____

Using our power to overcome and to become stronger _____

Knowing that with God all things are possible _____

Understanding that God believes we want to do better _____

Remembering the Church's history and connecting to the stories of other faithful people

_____

Valuing selflessness _____

Family Tree

Fill in the family tree as best you can. Start with you and your brothers and sisters, and go backward. How far back can you go?

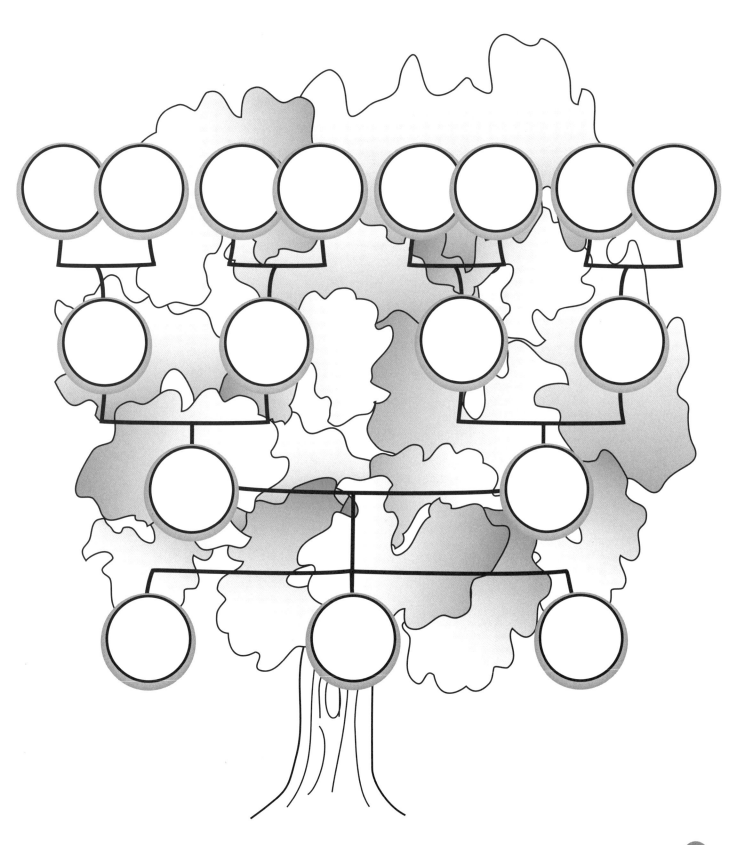

We Are Family

Use this list to write your personal history inside your person-outline:

- Define a talent and how you have used the talent (for better or for worse).
- Define a weakness and, if the weakness has been a problem, how you have overcome or learned from that weakness.
- Describe your faith and how you show it or live it.
- Name three important values that your parents taught you.
- Name three important hopes, dreams, or desires for the future.
- Describe a sacrifice you have made and how that sacrifice has affected you.
- List five words that describe you.

Reflection Questions

- Where can you see evidence of God's presence in your life?

- Where have you seen evidence of God's presence in the lives of others, your parents, your friends, other parishioners?

Extended Family

Name three members of your extended family—coaches, teachers, church leaders, adults, peers.

Letter to My Extended Family

Write a letter to one of the members of the extended family you listed on the previous activity, thanking that person for her or his support and encouragement.

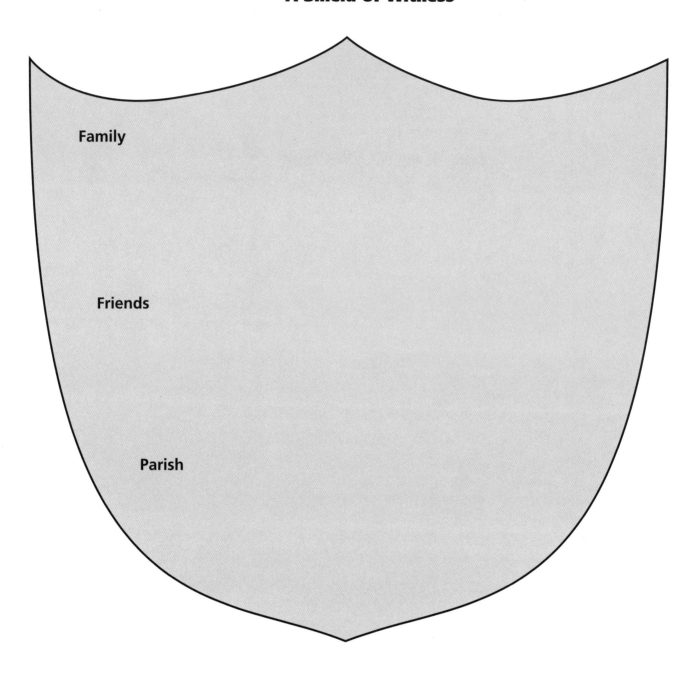

Family

Friends

Parish

Blessing of the Trees

Leader: Our response is, "Blessed be our God."

Leader: Blessed be the Simeons in our lives, who teach us patience.

All: Blessed be our God.

Leader: Blessed be the Annas in our lives, who teach us how to wait with joy.

All: Blessed be our God.

Leader: Blessed be the pilgrims in our lives, who teach us how to journey in faith.

All: Blessed be our God.

Leader: Blessed be parents and stepparents who shape us.

All: Blessed be our God.

Leader: Blessed be our relatives and friends who support us.

All: Blessed be our God.

Leader: Blessed be our extended family members for whom we are grateful.

All: Blessed be our God.

Leader: Blessed be this faith community. May we grow in wisdom, age, and grace.

All: Blessed be our God.

Canticle of Simeon

Master, now you are dismissing your servant in peace,
    according to your word,
for my eyes have seen your salvation,
    which you have prepared in the presence of all peoples,
a light for revelation to the Gentiles,
    and for glory to your people Israel.

(Luke 2:29–32)

Chapter 7
All Are Welcome

The Magi were kings of neighboring countries whose citizens practiced different religions. Amazingly, these Wise Men, who were not Jewish, traveled from afar to see the newborn King of the Jews! The Epiphany is the revelation that Christmas happened. This was the "aha" moment that tells us this was an incredible event. The Feast of the Epiphany reminds us that nothing is impossible with God. Because the Magi spent such effort to find and welcome Jesus, the Epiphany is a celebration that reminds Christians to open their hearts wide to the glory of God found in the birth of Jesus. The theme of this time is one of welcome and hospitality. The story of the Magi reminds Christians that they all travel on the road to meet Jesus and that sometimes they may feel like strangers in strange lands who need welcome and hospitality.

READINGS

Feast of the Epiphany

- **Cycle A, B, and C:** Isaiah 60:1–6,20; Ephesians 3:2–3,5–6; Matthew 2:1–12

STUDY IT!

The Magi Return Press Conference

What does this passage from Matthew tell us about our "interviewee"?

What three or four questions do we want to ask the other interviewees at the press conference?

1.

2.

3.

4.

We Are a Welcoming Community

Rules of Welcome

1. _____
_____

2. _____
_____

3. _____
_____

4. _____
_____

5. _____
_____

6. _____
_____

7. _____
_____

8. _____
_____

9. _____
_____

10. _____
_____

Welcome Pledge

PRAY IT!

Intercessions

Leader: For the stranger among us.

All: All are welcome.

Leader: For the outcast at the fringes.

All: All are welcome.

Leader: For refugees and migrants.

All: All are welcome.

Leader: For pilgrims and seekers.

All: All are welcome.

Leader: For the needy we do not see.

All: All are welcome.

Leader: For the lonely and different.

All: All are welcome.

Leader: For sinners and the selfish.

All: All are welcome.

Leader: For those who make us welcome.

All: All are welcome.

Chapter 8
Baptism of the Lord

Baptism is usually a formal celebration in the Catholic Church. Parents of the child being baptized choose godparents and invite family and friends to witness this sacrament of initiation. The white garment, the candle, the water, the oil—all are significant symbols. With Baptism, Christians are claimed by Christ and presented to the faithful community.

Jesus's baptism in the Jordan River was not quite as elaborate as the Baptisms we celebrate today. It was still very important. Jesus humbled himself to be like everyone else. His asking John to baptize him demonstrates this humility.

The Catholic faith challenges us to seek beyond first impressions, beyond what someone looks like, and even beyond actions and into the heart of the person. When we see each person as someone God created and loved, then we can challenge ourselves to truly appreciate each person.

READINGS

Baptism of the Lord

- **Cycle A:** Isaiah 42:1–4,6–7,21; Acts 10:34–38; Matthew 3:13–17
- **Cycle B:** Isaiah 42:1–4,6–7,21; Acts 10:34–38; Mark 1:7–11
- **Cycle C:** Isaiah 42:1–4,6–7,21; Acts 10:34–38; Luke 3:15–16,21–22

ICEBREAKER

Beyond First Impressions

1	2

Blessing

God of love, with the feast of the Baptism of our Lord, the Christmas season of our liturgical year comes to a close. We give thanks for the blessings of the season and for the promise of the year ahead of us. We gather to remember that, like Jesus, we are the beloved sons and daughters of God. Let us rejoice in one another and in God, our savior. Amen. (Janet Claussen and Marilyn Kielbasa, *Ministry Ideas for Celebrating Advent and Christmas with Teens, Families, and Parishes*, page 85)

Jesus Is Just Like Us

Use this space to list the verses about God's support and care for all people that your group found in the concordance, which is a book for locating words or phrases in the Scriptures.

Which of the Scripture verses you listed personally appeal to you?

MY FAVORITES

Peace Be with Us All

Leader: When we think of others and don't worry so much about ourselves,
All: Then peace will reign.
Leader: When we are careful about treating others the way that we want to be treated,
All: Then peace will reign.
Leader: When we reach out to others,
All: Then peace will reign.
Leader: When we rely on hope, even in desperate times,
All: Then peace will reign.
Leader: When we count on God to guide us,
All: Then peace will reign.
Leader: When we learn from Jesus's example,
All: Then peace will reign.
Leader: Blessed be this faith community. May we grow in wisdom, age, and grace.
All: Amen.
Leader: Peace be with you!
All: And also with you.
Leader: Let us all go in peace to love and serve God and one another.
All: Thanks be to God!

Chapter 9
Light for the World
Extended Activities

In ancient times, people used candles for the practical reason of providing light, but early Christians also attached a symbolic or spiritual meaning to candles. They used candles and light to remind the faithful that Christ is the light of the world and that his followers are called to be light for the world. While Christians are called to live in the light of Christ and to be a light for the world, they often create darkness by sin and selfishness. We must take time to reflect on the ways we sometimes create darkness in our lives and how we can become disciples who better live and reflect the light of Jesus.

ICEBREAKER   **Stories of Light**

Stories of Light	Me	My partner
No electricity in the house		
Baptism		
Birthday		
Easter Vigil		
Wedding		

There Is a Light

Leader: That we may overcome the darkness of fear.

All: Let our light shine.

Leader: That we may open our eyes and recognize the light of Christ in ourselves.

All: Let our light shine.

Leader: That we may not hide the light of Christ within us.

All: Let our light shine.

Leader: That we may unselfishly share the light of Christ, especially outside the Christmas season.

All: Let our light shine.

Leader: Let us pray.

God of light and God of darkness,
You made the sun for the day
and the stars and moon for the night
to guide the faithful pilgrim
as we journey in faith.
We long to rest in the joy of your Kingdom.
We come as seekers of your Light,
your Son, Jesus Christ.
We ask for courage to overcome the fears and angers
that prevent us from bearing witness to your Light,
We ask you to open eyes and open hearts,
so that we might always see and share the light of Christ.
We ask this through your Son and with the Holy Spirit.

All: Amen.

Christ Is Our Light

Take a few moments to write about a time when Christ was a light for you. Use the following questions to help you reflect:

When has Jesus been a light for you?

at home . . .

in school . . .

with friends . . .

with your family . . .

in a relationship . . .

Light Our Way Home

How can I be a light to others?
(Some examples are *keeping a neat room, helping around the house without being asked,* and *being patient with others.* Be creative in your responses.)

Additional Notes

Advent is celebrated during the four weeks before Christmas. Those four weeks give Christians time to reflect on the meaning of the Christmas season. It sure is easy to get wrapped up in worrying about the presents we hope to receive or when school will let out for break. But in the midst of the hustle and bustle, Advent gives us peace, calm, patience, and hope. Advent offers us a chance to practice thinking about other people. Advent can be a great time to consider gifts from the heart and not necessarily from the mall.

This book in the Journey of Faith series will be your companion as you journey through the seasons of Advent and Christmas. This time will remind you of two important journeys: Mary and Joseph's to Bethlehem and the Magi's (three kings) to visit Mary and Joseph after Jesus's birth. Their journeys remind us that God is always with us, always guiding us, and always caring about us. God's being with you is the most important thing you can take with you on your Advent journey.

Saint Mary's Press

Winona, Minnesota
www.smp.org

ISBN 0-88489-881-4

Marshmallowville

Town Hall

Marshmallowville

Author: Dianna Rembert

Illustrator: Dianna L. McKinney